Text and Illustrations copyright © 2013 by Karen M. Cauller

Published by Building Sandcastles, LLC

Reach us by mail at:
Building Sandcastles, LLC
P.O. Box 22704
Hilton Head Island, SC 29925

ISBN-10: 0-9859222-0-6
ISBN-13: 978-0-9859222-0-7

Printed in China

It's Still Your Turn

A Golf Day With Dad

WRITTEN BY KAREN CAULLER
ILLUSTRATED BY SARAH DIETSCHE

Building Sandcastles, LLC
Hilton Head Island, South Carolina

We went golfing, just Dad and me.
I had a yellow ball and Dad had
a white ball.

The cart had plenty of room for my new clubs and Dad's clubs. It also had room for boiled peanuts, pimento cheese sandwiches, and sweet tea.

Dad told me I could hit the ball first so I carefully put my ball on the first tee. "A fine shot," Dad chuckled.

Then I looked at the golf course map while Dad took a swing. His ball landed next to a large alligator.

"It's still your turn," I said.

The second hole had sand around it.

Dad took a fast swing.

The ball rolled into the sand.

He knew just what to do.
He kept swinging his club
until he dug a big hole.
"It's still your turn," I said.

On the third hole it began to get windy. Dad picked some grass and threw it up in the air to see which way the wind was blowing.

He hit his ball very high. We drove around and around and around trying to find his ball.
"It's still your turn," I said.

The fourth hole was in a swamp. I smelled the sweet jasmine while Dad took a swing.

His ball landed in the tall pampas grass by a snake. My Dad hopped back into the cart.

"It's still your turn," I said.

The fifth hole was by a black lagoon. I munched on boiled peanuts while Dad took a swing. His ball landed near a very still blue heron. When Dad tried to get close to his ball the blue heron made a loud noise and flapped its wings while flying away.

The sixth hole had many houses around it.
I watched the children jumping on a trampoline
in their back yard. Dad's ball went into a
swimming pool near a man floating on a raft.

The man yelled and took my Dad's ball
into his garage.
"It's still your turn," I said.

Clouds rolled in across the sky and it began to drizzle on the next hole.
Dad put on his rain slicker and rain pants.

I held an enormous red striped umbrella. Dad's ball hit a palm tree and bounced and bounced and bounced. We ran and hid behind the cart.
"It's still your turn," I said.

On the eighth hole the sun came out from behind a cloud and it got very hot. I took off my sweater. A lot of mosquitoes started buzzing around Dad's head.

"It's still your turn," I said.

On the ninth hole the snack cart stopped by to give us something to eat and drink. My Dad liked telling jokes to the lady driving the cart.

"It's still your turn," I said.

The next hole had lots of trees. I wrote on the scorecard while Dad took a swing. The ball landed in an old oak tree.

Dad tried to get his ball, but a lady saw him in her yard and got mad. She squirted my Dad with a water hose. My Dad fell into a leafy bush.

"It's still your turn," I said.

The eleventh hole needed only three shots to go into the cup. I sipped sweet tea while Dad took a swing. His ball landed next to the hole. A beautiful butterfly landed on the ball.

He waved the butterfly away, but the ball rolled away too. It began to roll faster and faster and faster until we could not see it anymore.

"It's still your turn," I said.

It was a long ride to the twelfth hole. I got a drink of cold water in a paper cup. Dad's ball hit a bench and bounced backward between his legs.

"It's still your turn," I said.

The next hole was very long. Dad took the number one club with the huge head out of his bag. He took a very big swing. It was so big that he missed the ball and fell onto the ground. I helped him stand back up.

"It's still your turn," I said.

The fourteenth hole had a rippling stream.
I unwrapped my pimento cheese sandwich
while Dad took a swing. His ball skipped across
the water and sank.

My Dad stretched his catcher to the ball and grabbed it. We tried to close the ball catcher. We pushed and pushed and pushed, but it would not go back together again.

"It's still your turn," I said.

The fifteenth hole was so wide that it looked like a park. I washed the balls while Dad took a swing. His ball landed in the middle of the grass.

A hairy dog came to play.
The dog put the ball in
his mouth and ran away.
"It's still your turn," I said.

On the sixteenth hole it began to get dark.
The water sprinklers came on and made
Dad all wet.

"It's still your turn," I said.

The next hole was in the woods. I looked up at the squirrels jumping across the branches in the tall trees. A pointy prickly pine cone fell on Dad's nose and made a red mark. "Ouch!" my dad yelled. **"It's still your turn," I said.**

The last hole was short and I could see the flag waving. My Dad grinned while he put his ball on the tee. The ball went right into the cup.

Clink! Clink! A hole-in-one!
"It's my turn now!" I yelled.

My dad and I went into the clubhouse to see his friends and to tell them about the hole-in-one. Dad was very happy. They laughed and told him that it didn't count because no one saw it but me.

But he didn't care. He said I was a big help. It was a good day after all, just me and my Dad.

GLOSSARY
CAN YOU FIND?

American Alligator

Typically black or dark brown with light yellow-white cross bands on the body. Can reach lengths up to 16 feet and weigh up to 1,000 pounds. They can live up to 30 to 50 years and inhabit swamps, streams, rivers, ponds, and lakes mainly in the southeastern US. They typically eat a wide variety of animals including fish, birds, snakes, turtles, amphibians, and mammals.

American Green Tree Frog

Grows up to 2.5 inches long. The bodies are usually shades of green from bright yellowish olive to lime green. They are found in the central and southeastern US. Habitats include small ponds, large lakes, and marshes. Likes to eat flies, mosquitoes, and other small insects.

Bald Eagle

It is the national bird of the United States. The plumage is brown with a white head and tail. It is not really bald. It is a bird of prey which feeds mainly on fish. It is found near large bodies of water. It builds the largest nest of any North American bird. The nest is up to 13 feet deep, 8.2 feet wide, and can weigh up to 1.1 ton.

Black Vulture

Has glossy black feathers, a featherless, grayish-black head and neck, and a short hooked beak. The wingspan is about 4 and 5 feet. It is a scavenger and feeds on carrion, but will also eat eggs or kill newborn animals. It also feeds at garbage dumps. It has keen eyesight and a keen sense of smell. It generally raises two chicks per year, which it feeds by regurgitation.

Bluebird

Adult males are bright blue on top and have a reddish brown throat and breast. Adult females have a lighter blue wings and tail, a brownish throat and breast and a grey crown and back. They are usually between 6.3 and 8.3 inches long, have a wingspan of 9.8 and 13 inches and weigh 0.95 – 1.2 ounces. They eat insects and berries. Gardeners like to attract blue birds because they quickly rid a garden of insect pests. They commonly use nest boxes or old woodpecker holes.

Cardinal

Often called "redbirds." Only the males have the red plumage. Female feathers are tan and gray. Cardinals sing a variety of different melodies. Males can be aggressive when defending their territory. They eat insects, seeds, grains, fruit, and sap.

Carolina Anole

This lizard is sometimes called the green anole or the American anole. Usually measures 6-8 inches long. Their diet consists of small insects and grasses. The coloration ranges from bright green to dark brown.

Coral Snake

A snake between 3 and 5 feet long. A popular saying to figure out if a snake is poisonous: "Red on black, friend of Jack, red on yellow, kill a fellow." It is very elusive. They have a pair of small fangs to deliver their venom. They have the most potent venom of any North American snake. They have a tendency to hold onto their victims when biting.

Dolphin

A marine mammal and are carnivores eating mostly fish and squid. The dolphin is among the most intelligent animals. They are social and live in pods of up to 12 dolphins. Dolphins are capable of making a broad range of sounds. They like to jump and play. The are found worldwide, mostly in shallower seas.

Great Blue Heron

Has gray-blue plumage and often stands motionless, but can move lightening fast to grab a fish. They have a long neck and legs with a large dagger-like bill. The head to tail length is 36 – 54 inches, wingspan is 66 – 79 inches, and has a height of 45 – 54 inches. It weighs 4.6 – 7.9 pounds.

Lagoon

Coastal shallow bodies of water connected to the ocean by inlets between barrier islands. Lagoons are found along more than 75% of the eastern and Gulf coasts. They are sensitive to changes in sea level.

Loblolly Pine Tree

Has dark green needles and grows up to 100 feet in height. The famous "Eisenhower Tree" is a loblolly pine. The tree is located at the 17th hole of Augusta National Golf Club. President Dwight D. Eisenhower hit the tree so many times that, at a 1956 club meeting, he proposed that it be cut down. Not wanting to offend the President, the club's chairman, Clifford Roberts, immediately adjourned the meeting rather than reject the request outright.

Malachite (Siproeta stelenes)

This butterfly is named after a beautiful green mineral, malachite. Its wingspan is between 3.3 and 3.9 inches. Adults feed on flower nectar, rotting fruit, dead animals, and bat dung. It is one of the few butterflies that can feed on both flowers and fruit.

Pelican

A large water bird which lives mainly on fish which it catches at or near the surface. It has a large beak and throat pouch used in catching its prey and draining water from the scooped up contents before swallowing. They live near inland and coastal waters. The length is 4.6 feet, wingspan is 6.6 – 7.5 feet, and the weight is 7.9 – 9.9 pounds.

White-Tailed Deer

Can run up to 40 miles per hour, jump 9 foot fences, and swim 13 miles per hour. The white underside of the deer's tail waves when running and is flashed when danger is sensed. The male deer weighs between 130 – 290 pounds and is known as a buck or stag. They regrow their antlers every year. The female deer weighs between 88 to 200 pounds and is known as a doe.

INFORMATION ABOUT THE:

AUTHOR

Karen Cauller is a reading specialist who lives on Hilton Head Island, SC. She is a graduate of Penn State University, West Chester University, and the University of South Carolina. Even though her son, Matthew, is now grown, she looks back fondly on his days as a "junior golfer."

ILLUSTRATOR

Sarah Dietsche is an artist and illustrator who lives on Hilton Head Island, SC with her husband, Joe, and three children (Aiden, Dylan, and Morgan). She is a graduate of Virginia Marti College of Art and Design. She loves all outdoor activities and enjoys nature.

GRAPHIC DESIGNER

Nicholas Maganini is a graphic designer who grew up on Hilton Head Island, SC. Nick is a gradute of Clemson University and when he's not designing he can be found in the air flying his hang glider and chasing hawks. If the skies aren't suitable, he can be found on a mountain wall rock climbing or on a bike riding the wooded trails of the upstate of South Carolina.

DEDICATION

To Pat and Matt with love.
To Stacy, Mike, Stephanie, and Brian for
their encouragement and support.

All of the events in this book have actually
happened at one time or another.